I O L A N T H E

or

The Peer and the Peri

Book by

W. S. GILBERT

Music by

ARTHUR SULLIVAN

Authentic Version Edited by

BRYCESON TREHARNE

This score contains all the dialogue

Ed. 1822

G. SCHIRMER, Inc.

DISTRIBUTED BY

HAL•LEONARD®

DRAMATIS PERSONAE

THE LORD CHANCELLOR

LORD MOUNTARARAT

LORD TOLLOLLER

PRIVATE WILLIS.................................*Of the Grenadier Guards*

STREPHON...*An Arcadian Shepherd*

QUEEN OF THE FAIRIES

IOLANTHE.....................................*A Fairy, Strephon's Mother*

CELIA.........⎫

LEILA.........⎬...*Fairies*

FLETA.........⎭

PHYLLIS.................*An Arcadian Shepherdess and Ward in Chancery*

CHORUS OF DUKES, MARQUISES, EARLS, VISCOUNTS, BARONS, AND FAIRIES

———————

ACT I—An Arcadian Landscape

ACT II—Palace Yard, Westminster

Date, between 1700 and 1882

ARGUMENT

Twenty-five years previous to the action of the opera, Iolanthe, a fairy, had committed the capital crime of marrying a mortal. The Queen of the Fairies had commuted the death sentence to banishment for life—on condition that Iolanthe must leave her husband without explanation and never see him again. Her son Strephon has grown up as a shepherd, half fairy, half mortal. Strephon loves Phyllis, a shepherdess who is also a Ward in Chancery; she returns his love, and knows nothing of his mixed origin.

At the beginning of the opera, the Queen is prevailed upon by other fairies to recall Iolanthe from exile. Strephon joins the glad reunion and announces his intention of marrying Phyllis in spite of the Lord Chancellor, her guardian, who refuses permission. The Queen approves, and plans to influence certain boroughs to elect Strephon to Parliament.

Meanwhile the entire House of Lords is enamored of Phyllis; they appeal in a body to the Lord Chancellor to give her to whichever peer she may select. The Lord Chancellor is also suffering the pangs of love, but feels he has no legal right to assign her to himself. Phyllis declines to marry a peer; Strephon pleads his cause in court again, but in vain. Iolanthe enters and holds tender converse with her son. Since she, like all fairies, looks like a girl of seventeen, Phyllis and the peers misinterpret the situation; they ridicule Strephon's claim that Iolanthe is his mother. Phyllis declares now that she will marry either Lord Mountararat or Lord Tolloller.

The Fairies take revenge by not merely sending Strephon to Parliament, but also influencing both Houses to pass any bills he may introduce. His innovations culminate in a bill to throw the peerage open to competitive examination. The Peers, seeing their doom approaching, appeal to the Fairies to desist. The Fairies have fallen in love with the Peers and would like to oblige, but it is too late to stop Strephon. The Queen reproaches her subjects for their feminine weakness; she acknowledges her own weakness for a sentry, Private Willis, but asserts that she has it under control.

Lord Mountararat and Lord Tolloller discover that if either marries Phyllis, family tradition will require the loser to kill his successful rival; both therefore renounce Phyllis in the name of friendship. The Lord Chancellor, after considerable struggle, pleads his own cause before himself and convinces himself that the law will allow him to marry her.

Meanwhile Strephon makes Phyllis understand that his mother is a fairy, and they are reconciled. They persuade Iolanthe to appeal to the Lord Chancellor. To make the appeal effective, she reveals her identity to him—her husband—and thus again incurs the death penalty. The other Fairies, however, have married their respective Peers, and announce to the Queen that they all have incurred the same sentence. The Lord Chancellor suggests the legal expedient of inserting a single word, to make the law read that every fairy who does *not* marry a mortal shall die. The Queen corrects the scroll, and asks Private Willis to save her life by marrying her. All the mortals present are then transformed into fairies and fly away with their consorts to Fairyland, leaving the House of Lords to be replenished according to intelligence rather than birth.

MUSICAL NUMBERS

Iolanthe
or
The Peer and the Peri

W. S. Gilbert

Arthur Sullivan

Overture

Act I

(Scene: *An Arcadian landscape. A river runs around the back of the stage. A rustic bridge crosses the river.*)

No. 1. Tripping hither, tripping thither
Opening Chorus and Soli
Celia, Leila, and Fairies

Celia and Chorus (SOP. I) *(They trip around the stage, singing as they dance.)*

Trip-ping hith-er, trip-ping thith-er, No-bod-y knows why or

Leila and Chorus (SOP. II)

Trip-ping hith-er, trip-ping thith-er, No-bod-y knows why or

whith-er, We must dance and we must

whith-er, We must dance and we must

sing ____ Round a - bout our fair - y ring. Trip-ping hith-er, trip-ping

sing ____ Round a - bout our fair - y ring. Trip-ping hith-er, trip-ping

thith-er, No - bod - y knows why or whith-er, We must dance and we must

thith-er, No - bod - y knows why or whith-er, We must dance and we must

sing Round a - bout our fair - y ring. Trip-ping hith-er, trip-ping

sing Round a - bout our fair - y ring. Trip-ping hith-er, trip-ping

dance and we must sing Round a - bout our fair - y

dance and we must sing Round a - bout our fair - y

E **Leila**
poco lento *a tempo*

ring. If you ask us how we live, Lov-ers all es - sen - tials give;

ring.

E *poco lento* *a tempo*

We can ride on lov - ers' sighs, Warm our - selves in lov - ers' eyes,

Bathe our - selves in lov - ers' tears, Clothe our - selves with lov - ers' fears,

18

Celia: Ah, it's all very well, but since our Queen banished Iolanthe, fairy revels have not been what they were.

Leila: Iolanthe was the life and soul of Fairyland. Why, she wrote all our songs and arranged all our dances! We sing her songs and we trip her measures, but we don't enjoy ourselves.

Fleta: To think that five-and-twenty years have elapsed since she was banished! What could she have done to have deserved so terrible a punishment?

Leila: Something awful! She married a mortal!

Fleta: Oh! Is it injudicious to marry a mortal?

Leila: Injudicious? It strikes at the root of the whole fairy system. By our laws, the fairy who marries a mortal dies.

Celia: But Iolanthe didn't die!

(Enter Queen of the Fairies.)

Queen: No, because your Queen, who loved her with a surpassing love, commuted her sentence to penal servitude for life, on condition that she left her husband without a word of explanation and never communicated with him again!

Leila: And that sentence of penal servitude she is now working out, on her head, at the bottom of that stream!

Queen: Yes, but when I banished her, I gave her all the pleasant places of the earth to dwell in. I'm sure I never intended that she should go and live at the bottom of a stream! It makes me perfectly wretched to think of the discomfort she must have undergone!

Leila: Think of the damp! And her chest was always delicate.

Queen: And the frogs! Ugh! I never shall enjoy any peace of mind until I know why Iolanthe went to live among the frogs!

Fleta: Then why not summon her and ask her?

Queen: Why? Because if I set eyes on her I should forgive her at once!

Celia: Then why not forgive her? Twenty-five years! it's a long time!

Leila: Think how we loved her!

Queen: Loved her? What was your love to mine? Why, she was invaluable to me! Who taught me to curl myself inside a buttercup? Iolanthe!—Who taught me to swing upon a cobweb? Iolanthe!—Who taught me to dive into a dewdrop, to nestle in a nutshell, to gambol upon gossamer? Iolanthe!

Leila: She certainly did surprising things!

Fleta: Oh, give her back to us, great Queen—for your sake, if not for ours!

(All kneel in supplication.)

Queen: *(irresolute)* Oh, I should be strong, but I am weak; I should be marble, but I am clay! Her punishment has been heavier than I intended. I did not mean that she should live among the frogs. And—Well! well! it shall be as you wish—it shall be as you wish!

No. 2. Invocation: Iolanthe! from thy dark exile

Soli and Chorus

Queen, Iolanthe, Celia, Leila, and Fairies

(Iolanthe rises from the water. She is clad in

water-weeds. She approaches the Queen with head bent and arms crossed.)

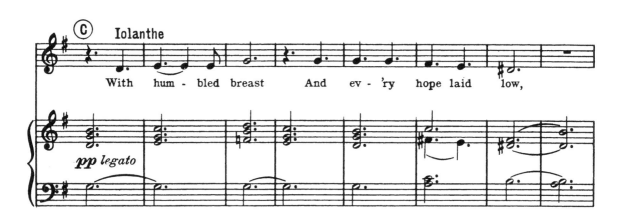

Iolanthe

With hum - bled breast   And ev - 'ry   hope laid   low,

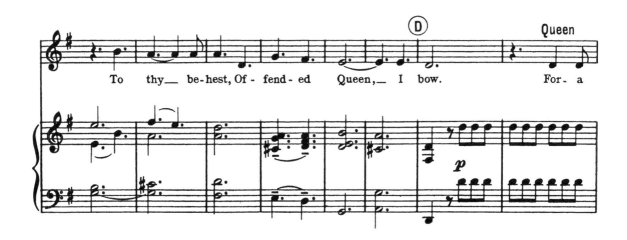

Queen

To   thy__ be-hest, Of - fend - ed   Queen,__ I bow.   For_ a

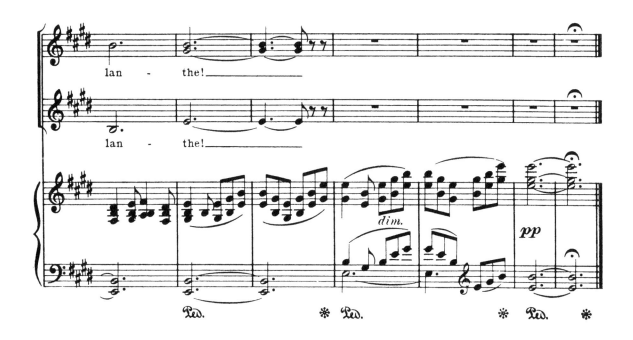

Queen: And now tell me: with all the world to choose from, why on earth did you decide to live at the bottom of that stream?

Iolanthe: To be near my son, Strephon.

Queen: Bless my heart! I didn't know you had a son.

Iolanthe: He was born soon after I left my husband by your royal command, but he doesn't even know of his father's existence.

Fleta: How old is he?

Iolanthe: Twenty-four.

Leila: Twenty-four! No one to look at you would think you had a son of twenty-four! But that's one of the advantages of being immortal — we never grow old Is he pretty?

Iolanthe: He's extremely pretty, but he's inclined to be stout.

All: (*disappointed*) Oh!

Queen: I see no objection to stoutness in moderation.

Celia: And what is he?

Iolanthe: He's an Arcadian shepherd, and he loves Phyllis, a Ward in Chancery.

Celia: A mere shepherd, and he half a fairy!

Iolanthe: He's a fairy down to the waist, but his legs are mortal.

Celia: Dear me!

Queen: I have no reason to suppose that I am more curious than other people, but I confess, I should like to see a person who is a fairy down to the waist, but whose legs are mortal.

Iolanthe: Nothing easier, for here he comes!

(Enter Strephon, singing and dancing and playing on a flageolet.
He does not see the Fairies, who retire up-stage as he enters.)

No. 3. Good morrow, good mother

Solo and Chorus

Strephon and Fairies

30

Iolanthe: Then the Lord Chancellor has at last given his consent to your marriage with his beautiful ward, Phyllis?

Strephon: Not he, indeed! To all my tearful prayers he answers me, "A shepherd lad is no fit helpmate for a ward of Chancery." I stood in court, and there I sang him songs of Arcadee, with flageolet accompaniment, in vain. At first he seemed a-mused, so did the Bar, but, quickly wearying of my song and pipe, he bade me get out. A servile usher then, in crumpled bands and rusty bombazine, led me, still singing, into Chancery Lane! I'll go no more; I'll marry her today, and brave the upshot, be what it may! — *(Sees Fairies)* But who are these?

Iolanthe: Oh, Strephon, rejoice with me; my Queen has pardoned me!

Strephon: Pardoned you, mother? This is good news, indeed!

Iolanthe: And these ladies are my beloved sisters.

Strephon: Your sisters? Then they are — my aunts. *(kneels)*

Queen: A pleasant piece of news for your bride on her wedding day!

Strephon: Hush! My bride knows nothing of my fairyhood. I dare not tell her, lest it frighten her. She thinks me mortal, and prefers me so.

Leila: Your fairyhood doesn't seem to have done you much good.

Strephon: Much good? My dear aunt! It's the curse of my existence! What's the use of being half a fairy? My body can creep through a keyhole, but what's the good of that when my legs are left kicking behind? I can make myself invisible down to the waist, but that's of no use when my legs remain exposed to view. My brain is a fairy brain, but from the waist downward I'm a gibbering idiot. My upper half is immortal, but my lower half grows older every day, and some day or other must die of old age. What's to become of my upper half when I've buried my lower half I really don't know.

Fairies: Poor fellow!

Queen: I see your difficulty, but with a fairy brain you should seek an intellectual sphere of action. Let me see: I've a borough or two at my disposal; would you like to go into Parliament?

Iolanthe: A fairy Member! That would be delightful.

Strephon: I'm afraid I should do no good there. You see, down to the waist I'm a Tory of the most determined description, but my legs are a couple of confounded Radicals, and on a division they'd be sure to take me into the wrong lobby. You see, they're two to one, which is a strong working majority.

Queen: Don't let that distress you; you shall be returned as a Liberal-Conservative, and your legs shall be our peculiar care.

Strephon: *(bowing)* I see your Majesty does not do things by halves.

Queen: No; we are fairies down to the feet.

No. 4. Fare thee well

Solo and Chorus

Queen and Fairies

ring. Trip-ping hith-er, trip-ping thith-er, We must

now be tak - ing wing To — an - oth - er

fair - y ring.

p stacc.

(Fairies and Queen trip off, Iolanthe, who

f *p*

takes an affectionate farewell of her son, going off last.)

No. 4a. Good morrow, good lover
Duet
Phyllis and Strephon

(Enter Phyllis, singing and dancing and accompanying herself on a flageolet.)

Allegretto

Phyllis

Good mor-row, good lov-er! ____ Good lov-er, good mor-row! ____

I prith-ee dis-cov-er, Steal, pur-chase, or bor-row

Some means of con-ceal-ing The care you are feel-ing, And

Strephon: *(embracing her)* My Phyllis! And today we're to be made happy for ever.

Phyllis: Well, we're to be married.

Strephon: It's the same thing.

Phyllis: I suppose it is. But oh, Strephon, I tremble at the step I'm taking! I believe it's penal servitude for life to marry a Ward of Court without the Lord Chancellor's consent. I shall be of age in two years. Don't you think you could wait two years?

Strephon: Two years! Have you ever looked in the glass?

Phyllis: No, never.

Strephon: Here, look at that *(showing her a pocket mirror)* and tell me if you think it's rational to expect me to wait two years?

Phyllis: *(looking at herself)* No; you're quite right; it's asking too much — one must be reasonable.

Strephon: Besides, who knows what will happen in two years? Why, you might fall in love with the Lord Chancellor himself by that time.

Phyllis: Yes, he's a clean old gentleman.

Strephon: As it is, half the House of Lords are sighing at your feet.

Phyllis: The House of Lords are certainly extremely attentive.

Strephon: Attentive? I should think they were! Why did five-and-twenty Liberal peers come down to shoot over your grass-plot last autumn? It couldn't have been the sparrows. Why did five-and-twenty Conservative peers come down to fish in your pond? Don't tell me it was the goldfish! No, no. Delays are dangerous, and if we are to marry, the sooner the better.

No. 5. None shall part us from each other
Duet
Phyllis and Strephon

38

(Exeunt Strephon and Phyllis together.)

(March. Enter Procession of Peers.)

No. 6. Entrance and March of Peers:
Loudly let the trumpet bray

Chorus, Tenors and Basses

Peers

44

Par - a - gons of ___ leg - is - la - tion,

Pil - lars__ of the__ Brit - ish__ na - tion.

Tan - tan - ta - ra, tan - ta - ra, Tzing, boom, tzing, boom, tan - ta - ra, Tzing, boom!

low - er mid - dle class-es, Bow, ye tradesmen, bow, ye mass-es, Bow, ye

low - er mid - dle class-es, Bow, ye tradesmen, bow, ye mass-es, Bow, ye

low - er mid - dle class-es, Bow, ye tradesmen, bow, ye mass - es. Tan - tan - ta -

low - er mid - dle class-es, Bow, ye tradesmen, bow, ye mass - es. Tan - tan - ta -

ra, tan - tan - ta - ra, tan - tan - ta - ra, tan - ta - ra, tan - ta -

ra, tan - tan - ta - ra, tan - tan - ta - ra, tan - ta - ra, tan - ta -

54

No. 7. The Law is the true embodiment

Song and Chorus

Lord Chancellor and Peers

(Enter the Lord Chancellor followed by his train-bearer.)

56

guard - ian I Of pret - ty young Wards in Chan - ce - ry, All ver - y a - gree - a - ble

girls, and none Are o - ver the age of twen - ty - one. A

pleas - ant oc - cu - pa - tion for A rath - er sus - cep - ti - ble Chan - cel - lor! A

Chorus of Peers

pleas - ant oc - cu - pa - tion for A rath - er sus - cep - ti - ble Chan - cel - lor!

58

Lord Chancellor

3. And ev - 'ry-one who'd

mar - ry a Ward Must come to me for my ac-cord, And in my court I

sit all day, Giv-ing a-gree-a-ble girls a-way, With

one for him— and one for he— And one for you— and one for ye— And

62

(Enter Lord Tolloller)

Ld. Toll. And now, my Lords, to the business of the day!

Ld. Chan: By all means. Phyllis, who is a Ward of Court, has so powerfully affected your Lordships that you have appealed to me in a body to give her to whichever one of you she may think proper to select; and a noble Lord has gone to her cottage to request her immediate attendance. It would be idle to deny that I, myself, have the misfortune to be singularly attracted by this young person. My regard for her is rapidly undermining my constitution. Three months ago I was a stout man. I need say no more. If I could reconcile it with my duty, I should unhesitatingly award her to myself, for I can conscientiously say that I know no man who is so well fitted to render her exceptionally happy.

Peers: Hear, hear!

Ld. Chan: But such an award would be open to misconstruction, and therefore, at whatever personal inconvenience, I waive my claim.

Ld. Toll. My Lord, I desire, on the part of this House, to express its sincere sympathy with your Lordship's most painful position.

Ld. Chan: I thank your Lordships. The feelings of a Lord Chancellor who is in love with a Ward of Court are not to be envied. What is his position? Can he give his own consent to his own marriage with his own Ward? Can he marry his own Ward without his own consent? And if he marries his own Ward without his own consent, can he commit himself for contempt of his own Court? And if he commit himself for contempt of his own Court, can he appear by counsel before himself to move for arrest of his own judgment? Ah, my Lords, it is indeed painful to have to sit upon a woolsack which is stuffed with such thorns as these!

(Enter Lord Mountarat)

Ld. Mount: My Lords, I have much pleasure in announcing that I have succeeded in inducing the the young person to present herself at the Bar of this House.

(Enter Phyllis)

No. 8. My well-loved lord and guardian dear
Trio and Chorus
Phyllis, Lord Tolloller, Lord Mountararat, and Peers

64

Par - ty we're sing - ing this song to!___ If you ask___ us dis-

tinct-ly to say, We re - ply___ with-out doubt or de-lay, The Par - ty we claim to be-

long to Is the Par - ty we're sing-ing this song to! The Par - ty we claim to be-

long to's The Par - ty we're sing-ing this song to!

Phyllis

I'm ver-y much pained to re- fuse, __ But I'll stick to my pipes and my

ta-bors, I can spell all the words that I use, __ And my gram-mar's as good as my

neigh-bours'. As for birth, I was born like the rest, __ My be - ha-viour is rus-tic but

heart-y, And I know where to turn for the best When I want a par-tic - u - lar Par - ty!

Segue No. 9

No. 9. Nay, tempt me not

Recitative and Chorus
Phyllis and Peers

Segue No. 10

No. 10. Spurn not the nobly born

Song and Chorus

Lord Tolloller and Peers

74

Nor with low-born dis-dain Aug - ment our tri - als; Hearts just as pure and fair

May beat in Bel-grave Square As in the low-ly air Of Sev-en Di - als!

Blue blood, blue blood! Of what a-vail art thou To

serve us now? Though dat-ing from the Flood, Blue blood, ah, blue blood!

76

Segue No. 11

No. 11. My Lords, it may not be

Recitative and Chorus

Phyllis, Lord Tolloller, Lord Mountarart, Strephon,
Lord Chancellor, and Peers

trothed are we, Be-trothed are we, And mean to be es-poused to-day!

trothed is he, Be-trothed is he, And means to be es-poused to-day!

trothed is he, Be-trothed is he, And means to be es-poused to-day!

(G) Lord Tol. *(aside, to each other)*

'Neath this blow, worse than stab of dag-ger, Though we mo-men-ta-ri-ly stag-ger,

Lord Mount. *(aside, to each other)*

'Neath this blow, worse than stab of dag-ger, Though we mo-men-ta-ri-ly stag-ger,

In each heart Proud are we in-nate-ly, Let's de-part, Dig-ni-fied and state-ly!

In each heart Proud are we in-nate-ly, Let's de-part, Dig-ni-fied and state-ly!

Chorus of Peers

Tan - ta - ra!

Tan - ta - ra!

(Exeunt all the Peers, marching round stage with much dignity. Lord Chancellor separates Phyllis from Strephon, and orders her off. She follows Peers. Manent Lord Chancellor and Strephon.)

Ld. Chan.: Now, sir, what excuse have you to offer for having disobeyed an order of the Court of Chancery?

Strephon: My lord, I know no Courts of Chancery; I go by Nature's Acts of Parliament. The bees, the breeze, the seas, the rooks, the brooks, the gales, the vales, the fountains, and the mountains, cry, "You love this maiden; take her, we command you!" 'Tis writ in heaven by the bright-barbed dart that leaps forth into lurid light from each grim thunder-cloud. The very rain pours forth her sad and sodden sympathy. When chorused Nature bids me take my love, shall I reply, "Nay, but a certain Chancellor forbids it"? Sir, you are England's Lord High Chancellor, but are you Chancellor of birds and trees, King of the winds and Prince of thunder-clouds?

Ld. Chan.: No. It's a nice point; I don't know that I ever met it before. But my difficulty is that at present there's no evidence before the Court that chorused Nature has interested herself in the matter.

Strephon: No evidence! You have my word for it. I tell you that she bade me take my love.

Ld. Chan.: Ah! but, my good sir, you mustn't tell us what she told you; it's not evidence. Now, an affidavit from a thunder-storm or a few words on oath from a heavy shower would meet with all the attention they deserve.

Strephon: And have you the heart to apply the prosaic rules of evidence to a case which bubbles over with poetical emotion?

Ld. Chan.: Distinctly. I have always kept my duty strictly before my eyes, and it is to that fact that I owe my advancement to my present distinguished position.

No. 12. When I went to the Bar as a very young man

Song

Lord Chancellor

86

never as-sume that a rogue or a thief Is a gen-tle-man wor-thy im-
learn-ed pro-fes-sion I'll nev-er dis-grace By tak-ing a fee with a

pli-cit be-lief, Be - cause his at-tor-ney has sent me a brief (Said
grin on my face, When I have-n't been there to at-tend to the case (Said

I to my-self— said I).
I to my-self— said I).

_p_

3. I'll nev-er throw dust in a ju-ry-man's eyes (Said
4. In oth-er pro-fes-sions in which men en-gage (Said

40989

I to my-self — said I), Or hood-wink a judge who is
I to my-self — said I), The Ar - my, the Na - vy, the

not o - ver-wise (Said I to my-self — said I), Or as -
Church, and the Stage (Said I to my-self — said I), Pro -

sume that the wit - ness - es sum - moned in force In Ex -
fes - sion - al li - cence, if car - ried too far, Your

che - quer, Queen's Bench, Com - mon Pleas, or Di - vorce, Have
chance of pro - mo - tion will cer - tain - ly mar — And I

per-jured them-selves as a mat-ter of course
fan-cy the rule might ap-ply to the Bar (Said I to my-self said

I!)

(Exit Lord Chancellor)

(Iolanthe enters)

Strephon: *(in tears)*
Oh, Phyllis! Phyllis! To be taken from you just as I was on the point of making you my own! Oh, it's too much! it's too much!

Iolanthe: My son in tears, and on his wedding-day!

Strephon: My wedding-day! Oh, mother, weep with me, for the law has interposed between us, and the Lord Chancellor has separated us for ever!

Iolanthe: The Lord Chancellor! — *(aside)* Oh, if he did but know!

Strephon: *(overhearing her)* If he did but know—what?

Iolanthe: No matter! The Lord Chancellor has no power over you. Remember, you are half a fairy; you can defy him—down to the waist.

Strephon: Yes, but from the waist downwards he can commit me to prison for years. Of what avail is it that my body is free, if my legs are working out seven years' penal servitude?

Iolanthe: True. But take heart: our Queen has promised you her special protection. I'll go to her and lay your peculiar case before her.

Strephon: My beloved mother! How can I repay the debt I owe you?

(As the Finale commences, the Peers appear at the back, advancing unseen and on tiptoe. Mountararat and Toll-oller lead Phyllis between them, who listens in horror to what she hears.)

No. 13. When darkly looms the day

Finale of Act I

Ensemble

(They point derisively to Iolanthe, laughing heartily at her. She clings for protection to Strephon.)

(Enter Lord Chancellor; Iolanthe veils herself.)

100

104

(Enter Fairies, tripping, headed by Celia, Leila, and Fleta, and followed by Queen.)

Chorus of Fairies

Trip-ping hith - er, trip - ping thith - er, No - bod - y knows why or whith - er; Why you want us we don't know, ___ But you've sum-moned us, and

110

Chorus of Fairies   **Ld. Chan.**

Ta-ra-did-dle, ta-ra-did-dle, tol lol lay! That fa-ble p'rhaps may serve his turn as

(aside)

well as an-y oth-er. I did-n't see her face, but if they

fon-dled one an-oth-er, And she's but sev-en-teen— I don't be-

lieve it was his moth-er! Ta-ra-did-dle, ta-ra-did-dle!

114

that's a kind of moth-er that is u-su-al-ly spu-rious!

that's a kind of moth-er that is u-su-al-ly spu-rious!

f unis. Ta-ra-did-dle, ta-ra-did-dle, tol lol lay!

f unis. Ta-ra-did-dle, ta-ra-did-dle, tol lol lay!

Allegro vivace ♩.=69
Ld. Chan.

Go a-way, mad-am, I should say, mad-am, You dis-

play, mad-am, Shock-ing taste. It is rude, mad-am, To in-trude, mad-am, With your

brood, mad-am, Bra-zen-faced! You come here, mad-am, In-ter-fere, mad-am, With a

peer, mad-am, (I am one.) You're a-ware, mad-am, What you dare, mad-am, So take

care, mad-am, And be-gone! Let us stay, mad-am; I should say, mad-am, They dis-

X

Chorus of Fairies *(to Queen)*

118

mor - tals! I will launch from fair - y

por - tals All ____ the most ____ ter - rif - ic thun-ders

In ____ my ____ ar - mor - y ____ of ____ won-ders! Should they

Phyllis *(aside)*

launch ter - rif - ic won-ders, All ____ would then ____ re -

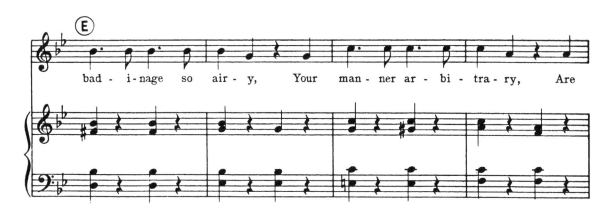

bad - i - nage so air - y, Your man - ner ar - bi - tra - ry, Are

out of place When face to face With an in - flu - en - tial Fair - y!

Lord Chan.

Chorus of Men
TENORS *p* (aside)

We nev-er knew We were talk-ing to An in-flu - en-tial Fair-y!
BASSES *p* (aside)

We nev-er knew We were talk-ing to An in-flu - en-tial Fair-y!

129

132

kind for-bear-ance they must claim, If they'd es-cape In an - y shape A

ver - y pain-ful wrench.

Your pow'rs we daunt-less - ly pooh-pooh: A dire re-venge will

(The word *"pres-tige"* is French, The

fall on you If you be-siege Our high *pres-tige.*

138

fy! You won't, you won't de - fy, You won't, you won't de -

fy! We thus, we thus de - fy, We thus, we thus de -

fy! _____

fy! _____

ff

(Fairies threaten Peers with their wands. Peers kneel as begging for mercy. Phyllis
implores Strephon to relent. He casts her from him, and she falls fainting into the arms
of Lord Mountararat and Lord Tolloller.)

Ped.

End of Act I

(Scene: *Palace Yard, Westminster. Westminster Hall, L. Clock Tower up R. C. Private Willis discov-*
ered on Sentry, R. Moonlight.)

No. 14. When all night long a chap remains

Song

Private Willis

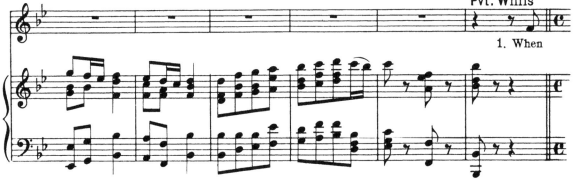

No. 15. Strephon's a Member of Parliament

Chorus

Fairies and Peers

148

Some-how no-bod-y now re-fus - es.

Whigs and To - ries Dim their glo - ries, Giv-ing an ear — to

all his sto - ries, Car-ry-ing ev - 'ry bill he may wish:

Here's a pret - ty ket-tle of fish! Ket-tle of fish— Ket-tle of fish—

(Enter Lords Tolloller and Mountararat from Westminster Hall.)

Celia: You seem annoyed.

Ld. Mount.: Annoyed! I should think so! Why, this ridiculous *protégé* of yours is playing the deuce with everything! Tonight is the second reading of his bill to throw the Peerage open to Competitive Examination!

Ld. Toll.: And he'll carry it, too!

Ld. Mount.: Carry it? Of course he will! He's a Parliamentary Pickford—he carries everything!

Leila: Yes. If you please, that's our fault.

Ld. Mount.: The deuce it is!

Celia: Yes; we influence the members, and compel them to vote just as he wishes them to.

Leila: It's our system; it shortens the debates.

Ld. Toll.: Well, but think what it all means! I don't so much mind for myself, but with a House of Peers with no grandfathers worth mentioning, the country must go to the dogs!

Leila: I suppose it must!

Ld. Mount.: I don't want to say a word against brains—I've a great respect for brains; I often wish I had some myself—but with a House of Peers composed exclusively of people of intellect, what's to become of the House of Commons?

Leila: I never thought of that.

Ld. Mount.: This comes of women interfering in politics. It so happens that if there is an institution in Great Britain which is not susceptible of any improvement at all, it is the House of Peers.

No. 16. When Britain really ruled the waves

Song and Chorus

Lord Mountararat, Fairies, and Peers

154

Leila: *(who has been much attracted by the Peers during the song)* Charming persons, are they not?

Celia: Distinctly. For self-contained dignity, combined with airy condescension, give me a British Representative Peer!

Ld. Toll.: Then, pray, stop this *protégé* of yours before it's too late. Think of the mischief you're doing!

Leila: *(crying)* But we *can't* stop him now. *(Aside to Celia)* Aren't they lovely? *(Aloud)* Oh, why did you go and defy us, you great geese?

No. 17. In vain to us you plead

Soli and Chorus

Leila, Celia, Fairies, Lord Mountararat, and Lord Tolloller

(Exeunt Mountararat and Tolloller and Peers. Fairies gaze wistfully after them. Enter Fairy Queen.)

Queen: Oh, shame! shame upon you! Is this your fidelity to the laws you are bound to obey? Know ye not that it is death to marry a mortal?

Leila: Yes; but it's not death to *wish* to marry a mortal.

Fleta: If it were, you'd have to execute us all.

Queen: Oh, this is weakness! Subdue it!

Celia: We know it's weakness, but the weakness is so strong!

Leila: We are not all as tough as you are!

Queen: Tough? Do you suppose that I am insensible to the effect of manly beauty? Look at that man *(referring to Pvt. Willis)*. A perfect picture! — *(to Pvt. Willis)* Who are you, sir?

Pvt. Willis: *(coming to "attention")* Private Willis, B Company, First Grenadier Guards.

Queen: You're a very fine fellow, sir.

Pvt. Willis: I am generally admired.

Queen: I can quite understand it. — *(To Fairies)* Now, here is a man whose physical attributes are simply godlike. That man has a most extraordinary effect upon me. If I yielded to a natural impulse I should fall down and worship that man. But I mortify this inclination; I wrestle with it, and it lies beneath my feet. That is how I treat my regard for that man!

No. 18. Oh, foolish fay

Song and Chorus

Queen and Fairies

This heart of mine Is soft as thine, Al-though I dare not say so!
Could thy Bri-gade With cold cas-cade Quench my great love, I won - der!

I won - der!

(Exeunt Fairies sorrowfully, headed by Fairy Queen.)

(Enter Phyllis.)

Phyllis: *(half crying)* I can't think why I'm not in better spirits. I'm engaged to two noblemen at once. That ought to be enough to make any girl happy; but I'm miserable. Don't suppose it's because I care for Strephon, for I hate him! No girl could care for a man who goes about with a mother considerably younger than himself.

(Enter Lord Mountararat and Lord Tolloller.)

Ld. Mount.: Phyllis, my darling!

Ld. Toll.: Phyllis! my own!

Phyllis: Don't! How dare you? But perhaps you're the two noblemen I'm engaged to?

Ld. Mount.: I am one of them.

Ld. Toll.: I am the other.

Phyllis: Oh, then, my darling! *(to Lord Mountararat)* My own! *(to Lord Tolloller)* Well, have you settled which it's to be?

Ld. Toll.: Not altogether; it's a difficult position. It would be hardly delicate to toss up. On the whole, we would rather leave it to you.

Phyllis: How can it possibly concern me? You are both earls, and you are both rich, and you are both plain.

Ld. Mount.: So we are. At least I am.

Ld. Toll.: So am I.

Ld. Mount.: No, no!

Ld. Toll.: Oh, I am indeed very plain.

Ld. Mount.: Well, well! perhaps you are.

Phyllis: There's really nothing to choose between you. If one of you would forego his title and distribute his estates among his Irish tenantry, why, then I should see a reason for accepting the other. *(Phyllis retires up.)*

Ld. Mount.: Tolloller, are you prepared to make this sacrifice?

Ld. Toll.: No!

Ld. Mount.: Not even to oblige a lady?

Ld. Toll.: No! not even to oblige a lady.

Ld. Mount.: Then the only question is, which of us shall give way to the other? Perhaps, on the whole, she would be happier with me. I don't know; I may be wrong.

Ld. Toll.: No, I don't know that you are. I really believe she would. But the awkward part of the thing is, that if you rob me of the girl of my heart, we must fight, and one of us must die. It's a family tradition that I have sworn to respect. It's a painful position, for I have a very strong regard for you, George.

Ld. Mount.: *(much affected)* My dear Thomas!

Ld. Toll.: You are very dear to me, George. We were boys together—at least *I* was. If I were to survive you, my existence would be hopelessly embittered.

Ld. Mount.: Then, my dear Thomas, you must not do it. I say it again and again: if it will have this effect on you, you must not do it. No, no! If one of us is to destroy the other, let it be me!

Ld. Toll.: No, no!

Ld. Mount.: Ah, yes! By our boyish friendship I implore you.

Ld. Toll. *(much moved)* Well! well! be it so. But no, no! I cannot consent to an act which would crush you with unavailing remorse.

Ld. Mount.: But it would not do so. I should be very sad at first—oh! who would not be?— but it would wear off. I like you *very much* but not, perhaps, as much as you like me.

Ld. Toll.: George, you're a noble fellow, but that tell-tale tear betrays you. No, George, you are very fond of me, and I cannot consent to give you a week's uneasiness on my account.

Ld. Mount.: But, dear Thomas, it would not last a week. Remember, you lead the House of Lords; on your demise I shall take your place. Oh, Thomas, it would not last a day!

Phyllis: *(coming down)* Now, I do hope you're not going to fight about me, because it really isn't worth while.

Ld. Toll.: *(looking at her)* Well, I don't believe it is.

Ld. Mount.: Nor I. The sacred ties of friendship are paramount.

No. 19. Though p'rhaps I may incur your blame

Quartet

Phyllis, Lord Tolloller, Lord Mountararat, and Private Willis

rank, and fame! But no one yet, in the world so wide, Has yield-ed up a

rank, and fame! But no one yet, in the world so wide, Has yield-ed up a

rank, and fame! But no one yet, in the world so wide, Has yield-ed up a

rank, and fame! But no one yet, in the world so wide, Has yield-ed up a

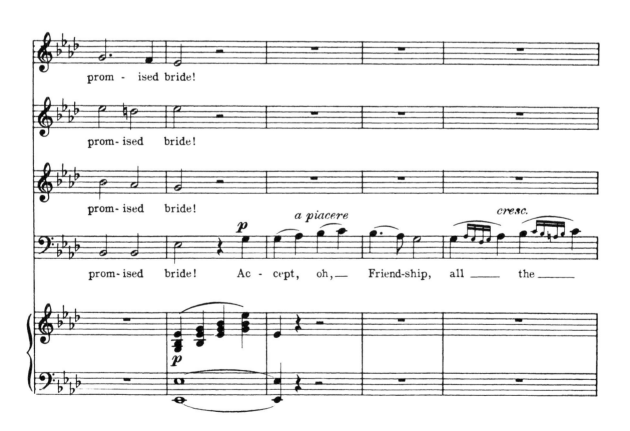

prom - ised bride!

prom-ised bride!

prom-ised bride!

prom-ised bride! Ac-cept, oh,— Friend-ship, all —— the ——

(Exeunt Lord Mountararat and Lord Tolloller, lovingly in one direction, Phyllis in another. Exit Sentry.)

No. 20. Love, unrequited, robs me of my rest

Recitative and Song

Lord Chancellor

(Enter Lord Chancellor, very miserable.)

Allegro ♩.=126

Recit.
Lord. Chan.

Love, un-re-quit-ed, robs me of my rest:

a tempo

Love, hope-less love, my ar-dent soul en-cum-bers:

169

ground in a heap, and you pick 'em all up in a tan-gle; Next your

pil-low re-signs and po-lite-ly de-clines to re-main at its u-su-al

an-gle! Well, you get some re-pose in the form of a doze, with hot

eye-balls and head ev-er ach-ing, But your slum-ber-ing teems with such

horrible dreams that you'd very much better be waking; For you

G dream you are crossing the Channel, and tossing about in a steamer from

Harwich— Which is something between a large bathing machine and a

very small second-class carriage— And you're giving a treat (penny

ice and cold meat) to a par-ty of friends and re - la-tions— They're a

rav- en-ous horde—and they all came on board at Sloane Square and South Ken-sing-ton

Sta-tions. And bound on that jour-ney you find your at - tor-ney (who

start- ed that morn-ing from Dev - on); He's a bit un-der-siz'd, and you

throw up your hand, and you find you're as cold as an i-ci-cle; In your

shirt and your socks (the black silk with gold clocks), cross-ing Sal's-bu-ry Plain on a

bi-cy-cle: And he and the crew are on bi-cy-cles too—which they've

some-how or oth-er in-vest-ed in— And he's tell-ing the tars all the

176

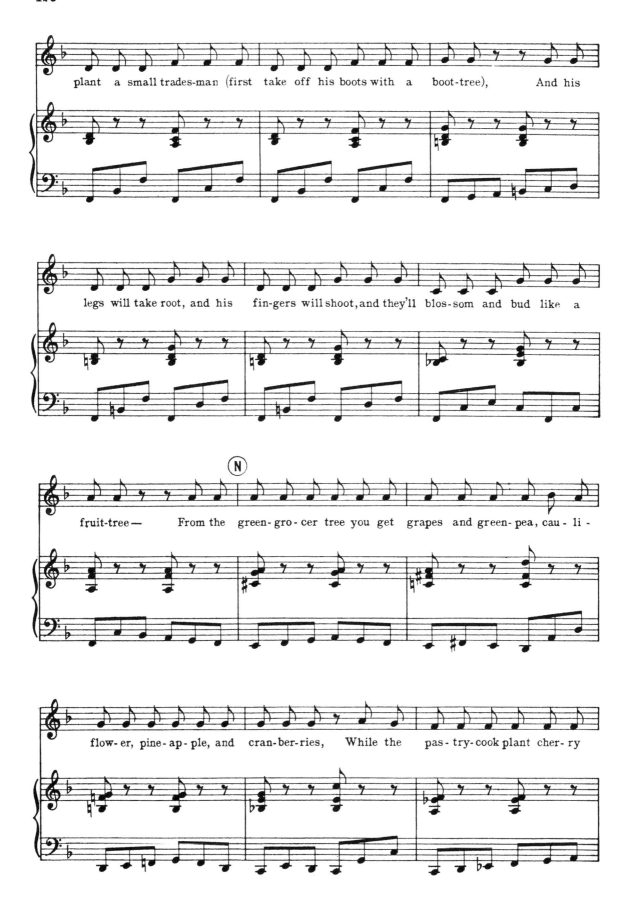

gen-er-al sense that you have-n't been sleep-ing in clo-ver;

But the dark-ness has pass'd, and it's day-light at

last, and the night has been long— dit-to, dit-to my

song— And thank good-ness they're both of them o-

(Lord Chancellor falls exhausted on a seat.)

ver! Con fuoco

(Lords Mountararat and Tolloller come forward.)

Ld. Mount.: I am much distressed to see your Lordship in this condition.

Ld. Chan.: Ah, my Lords, it is seldom that a Lord Chancellor has reason to envy the position of another, but I am free to confess that I would rather be two earls engaged to Phyllis than any other half-dozen noblemen upon the face of the globe.

Ld. Toll.: *(without enthusiasm)* Yes. It's an enviable position when you're the only one.

Ld. Mount.: Oh, yes — no doubt most enviable. At the same time, seeing you thus, we naturally say to ourselves, "This is very sad. His Lordship is constitutionally as blithe as a bird — he trills upon the bench like a thing of song and gladness. His series of judgments in F sharp, given *andante* in six-eight time, are among the most remarkable effects ever produced in a Court of Chancery. He is, perhaps, the only living instance of a judge whose decrees have received the honor of a double encore. How can we bring ourselves to do that which will deprive the Court of Chancery of one of its most attractive features?"

Ld. Chan.: I feel the force of your remarks, but I am here in two capacities, and they clash, my Lord, they clash! I deeply grieve to say that in declining to entertain my last application to myself, I presumed to address myself in terms which render it impossible for me ever to apply to myself again. It was a most painful scene, my Lord, most painful!

Ld. Toll.: This is what it is to have two capacities! Let us be thankful that we are persons of no capacity whatever.

Ld. Mount.: Come, come. Remember, you are a very just and kindly old gentleman, and you need have no hesitation in approaching yourself, so that you do so respectfully and with a proper show of deference.

Ld. Chan.: Do you really think so?

Ld. Mount.: I do.

Ld. Chan.: Well, I will nerve myself to another effort, and if that fails I resign myself to my fate.

No. 21. He who shies at such a prize

Trio

Lord Tolloller, Lord Mountararat, and Lord Chancellor

188

in for a pound— It's Love that makes the world go round!

in for a pound— It's Love that makes the world go round!

in for a pound— It's Love that makes the world go round!

(Dance, and exeunt arm-in-arm together.)

188

(Enter Strephon, in very low spirits.)

Strephon: I suppose one ought to enjoy oneself in Parliament when one leads both Parties, as I do! But I'm miserable, poor, broken-hearted fool that I am! Oh, Phyllis, Phyllis!—

(Enter Phyllis)

Phyllis: Yes.

Strephon: *(surprised)* Phyllis! But I suppose I should say, "My Lady". I have not yet been informed which title your ladyship has pleased to select.

Phyllis: I—I haven't quite decided. You see, *I* have no *mother* to advise *me!*

Strephon: No; I have.

Phyllis: Yes, a *young* mother.

Strephon: Not very—a couple of centuries or so.

Phyllis: Oh, she wears well.

Strephon: She does, she's a fairy.

Phyllis: I beg your pardon—a what?

Strephon: Oh, I've no longer any reason to conceal the fact—she's a fairy.

Phyllis: A fairy! Well, but—that would account for a good many things. Then I suppose *you're* a fairy.

Strephon: I'm half a fairy.

Phyllis: Which half?

Strephon: The upper half—down to the waistcoat.

Phyllis: Dear me! *(prodding him with her fingers)* There is nothing to show it.

Strephon: Don't do that.

Phyllis: But why didn't you tell me this before?

Strephon: I thought you would take a dislike to me. But as it's all off, you may as well know the truth—I'm only half a mortal.

Phyllis: *(crying)* But I'd rather have half a mortal I do love than half a dozen I don't.

Strephon: Oh, I think not. Go to your half dozen.

Phyllis: *(crying)* It's only two, and I hate 'em! Please forgive me.

Strephon: I don't think I ought to. Besides, all sorts of difficulties will arise. You know my grandmother looks quite as young as my mother. So do all my aunts.

Phyllis: I quite understand. Whenever I see you kissing a very young lady I shall know it's an elderly relative.

Strephon: You will? Then, Phyllis, I think we shall be very happy. *(embracing her)*

Phyllis: We won't wait long.

Strephon: No. We might change our minds. We'll get married first.

Phyllis: And change our minds afterwards?

Strephon: That's the usual course.

No. 22. If we're weak enough to tarry

Duet

Phyllis and Strephon

Allegro giocoso ♩.=138

Strephon

If we're weak e-nough to tar-ry Ere we mar-ry, You and I,

Of the feel-ing I in-spire You may tire___ By___ and by;

Ⓐ

For peers with flow-ing cof-fers Press their of-fers, That is why

190

Phyllis: But does your mother know you're — I mean, is she aware of our engagement?
(Enter Iolanthe)

Iolanthe: She is, and thus she welcomes her daughter-in-law. *(Kisses her.)*

Phyllis: She kisses just like other people! But the Lord Chancellor?

Strephon: I forgot him!—Mother, none can resist your fairy eloquence. You will go to him and plead for us?

Iolanthe: *(much agitated)* No, no! impossible!

Strephon: But our happiness, our very lives, depend upon our obtaining his consent!

Phyllis: Oh, madam, you cannot refuse to do this!

Iolanthe: You know not what you ask! The Lord Chancellor is — my husband!

Strephon: } Your husband?
Phyllis:

Iolanthe: My husband and your father! *(Addressing Strephon, who is much moved)*

Phyllis: Then our course is plain. On his learning that Strephon is his son, all objections to our marriage will be at once removed.

Iolanthe: Nay, he must never know. He believes me to have died childless; and, dearly as I love him, I am bound, under penalty of death, not to deceive him. But see, he comes! Quick, my veil!

(Iolanthe veils herself. Strephon and Phyllis go off on tiptoe. Enter Lord Chancellor)

Ld. Chan.: Victory! victory! Success has crowned my efforts, and I may consider myself engaged to Phyllis. At first I wouldn't hear of it; it was out of the question. But I took heart. I pointed out to myself that I was no stranger to myself—that, in point of fact, I had been personally acquainted with myself for some years. This had its effect. I admitted that I had watched my professional advancement with considerable interest, and I handsomely added that I yielded to no one in admiration for my private and professional virtues. This was a great point gained. I then endeavored to work upon my feelings. Conceive my joy when I distinctly perceived a tear glistening in my own eye! Eventually, after a severe struggle with myself, I reluctantly, most reluctantly, consented.

(Iolanthe comes down, veiled)

No. 23. My lord, a suppliant at your feet
Recitative and Ballad
Iolanthe

Andante non troppo lento ♩=76

He loves! If in the by-gone years Thine eyes have ev - er shed Tears—

bit - ter, un - a - vail - ing tears— For one un-time - ly dead—

If, in the e - ven - tide of life, Sad thoughts of her a - rise, Then

let the mem - 'ry of thy wife Plead for my boy— he dies! He

dies! If fond-ly laid a - side In some old cab - in - et, Me -

mo - rials of thy long - dead bride Lie, dear - ly trea-sured yet,

Then let her hal - low'd bri - dal dress— Her lit-tle daint - y gloves—Her

with-er'd flow'rs— her fad-ed tress— Plead for my boy— he loves!

(The Lord Chancellor is moved by this appeal. After a pause—)

No. 24. It may not be

Recitative

Iolanthe, Queen, Lord Chancellor, and Fairies

201

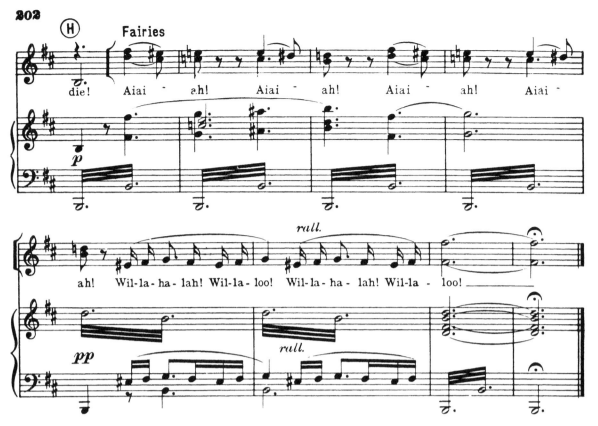

die! Aiai - ah! Aiai - ah! Aiai - ah! Aiai -

ah! Wil-la-ha-lah! Wil-la-loo! Wil-la-ha-lah! Wil-la - loo!_____

(The Peers and Strephon enter. The Queen raises her spear.)

Leila: Hold! If Iolanthe must die, so must we all, for as she has sinned, so have we!

Queen: What?

Celia: We are all fairy duchesses, marchionesses, countesses, viscountesses, and baronesses.

Ld.Mount.: It's our fault; they couldn't help themselves.

Queen: It seems they *have* helped themselves, and pretty freely too! —*(After a pause)* You have all incurred death, but I can't slaughter the whole company. And yet *(unfolding a scroll)* the law is clear: Every fairy must die who marries a mortal!

Ld.Chan.: Allow me, as an old Equity draughtsman, to make a suggestion. The subtleties of the legal mind are equal to the emergency. The thing is really quite simple; the insertion of a single word will do it. Let it stand that every fairy shall die who *does'nt* marry a mortal, and there you are, out of your difficulty at once!

Queen: We like your humor. Very well. *(Altering the MS. in pencil)* —Private Willis!

Pvt.Willis: *(coming forward)* Ma'am?

Queen: To save my life it is necessary that I marry at once. How should you like to be a fairy guardsman?

Pvt.Willis: Well, ma'am, I don't think much of the British soldier who wouldn't ill-convenience himself to save a female in distress.

Queen: You are a brave fellow. You're a fairy from this moment. *(Wings spring from Sentry's shoulders.)* —And you, my lords, how say you? Will you join our ranks?

(Fairies kneel to Peers, and implore them to do so. Phyllis and Strephon enter.)

Ld.Mount.: *(to Tolloller)* Well, now that the Peers are to be recruited entirely from persons of intelligence, I really don't see what use *we* are down here, do you, Tolloller?

Ld.Toll.: None, whatever.

Queen: Good! *(Wings spring from the shoulders of Peers.)* —Then away we go to Fairyland!

No. 25. Soon as we may, off and away

Finale

Ensemble

206

208

End of Opera